VIEWS

WASHINGTON

A COLLECTION OF PHOTOGRAPHS
BY CHRIS JACOBSON

EMERALD POINT PRESS
an imprint of

Thunder Bay Press

ISBN 10: 0 9637816 2 6
ISBN 13: 978 0 9637816 2 8

Copyright © 2006
Thunder Bay Press, Holt, Michigan

Copyright © 2005
Emerald Point Press, Seattle, Washington
An imprint of Thunder Bay Press

Cover:
Sunset at First Beach, La Push, Washington

Printed in China

MOUNT BAKER FROM ARTIST POINT

FALL COLORS, UNIVERSITY OF WASHINGTON ARBORETUM

BOARDWALK TRAIL, LAKE OZETTE

SPRING COLORS, UNIVERSITY OF WASHINGTON ARBORETUM

SNOWY EGRET

WETLANDS, UNIVERSITY OF WASHINGTON ARBORETUM

MOUNT RAINIER FROM UPPER REFLECTION LAKE

LAUGHINGWATER CREEK, OHANAPECOSH

Ross Lake, North Cascades National Park

THE PINNACLES, NORTH CASCADES NATIONAL PARK

SAN JUAN ISLANDS FROM MOUNT ERIE

SEATTLE FROM KERRY PARK ON QUEEN ANNE HILL

SEA STACKS AT FIRST BEACH, LA PUSH

TUG BOAT IN THE MIST, GIG HARBOR

MOUNT SHUKSAN FROM PICTURE LAKE

MOUNT RAINIER FROM KERRY PARK ON QUEEN ANNE HILL

SEATTLE AND THE OLYMPICS FROM SOMMERSET HILL

MOUNT RAINIER FROM PARADISE

SPRING FLOWERS, MOUNT VERNON

SEATTLE AND THE OLYMPICS FROM SOMMERSET HILL

PIKE PLACE PUBLIC MARKET, SEATTLE

CAMELLIA, UNIVERSITY OF WASHINGTON ARBORETUM

Tulip fields, Mount Vernon

SEATTLE FROM ALKI BEACH

MOUNT RAINIER AND PUGET SOUND FROM MAGNOLIA PARK

DENNY CREEK NEAR SNOQUALMIE PASS

MOUNT RAINIER FROM PARADISE

LIME KILN LIGHTHOUSE, SAN JUAN ISLAND

CITY PARK AND BELLEVUE SKYLINE

Fall colors, University of Washington Arboretum

PALOUSE WHEAT FIELDS FROM STEPTOE BUTTE

GOLD CREEK POND NEAR SNOQUALMIE PASS

Mount Rainier and Eunice Lake from Tolmie Point

POND WITH LEAVES, UNIVERSITY OF WASHINGTON ARBORETUM

Tulip fields, Mount Vernon

MOUNT RAINIER FROM EDITH CREEK

DENNY CREEK NEAR SNOQUALMIE PASS

FALL COLORS, UNIVERSITY OF WASHINGTON ARBORETUM

MOUNT SHUKSAN FROM PICTURE LAKE

Sea Stacks at First Beach, La Push

MOUNT RAINIER FROM UPPER REFLECTION LAKE

Gig Harbor Marina

Bathing rocks at Denny Creek near Snoqualmie Pass

COASTLINE, OLYMPIC NATIONAL PARK

Franklin Falls near Snoqaulmie Pass

MOUNT RAINIER FROM REFLECTION LAKES